PEKING OPERA

Text by Rewi Alley
Pictures by Eva Siao
          Weng Naiqiang
          Zhang Zudao
          Di Xianghua and Others

NEW WORLD PRESS
Beijing, China

First Edition 1984
Second Printing 1989
Editor: Ma Jie
Art Editor: Li Yuhong

ISBN 7-80005-090-4/J.019

Published by
NEW WORLD PRESS
24 Baiwanzhuang Road, Beijing, China

Distributed by
China International Book Trading Corporation
P.O. Box 399, Beijing, China Postal Zone: 100044

Printed in the People's Republic of China

PREFACE

In China the opera has occupied a very unique position. It is a position that has not been vacated up to this present day for, in spite of the patronage by the wealthy, men of letters, and officials in the past, it has always been an art of the people. To understand something of China, one must surely try to understand some of the highlights of the stage, especially of Peking Opera.

These lines have been written to accompany the very human pictures that Eva Siao has taken of Peking Opera. This album was first published by New World Press in 1957. The photos were almost entirely in black and white. This present edition is in colour and has recent photos taken by Eva Siao and those by the photographers Weng Naiqiang, Zhang Zudao, Di Xianghua and others.

As was the case with every facet of traditional Chinese culture, Peking Opera had a difficult time during the "cultural revolution", which lasted from 1966 through the fall of the Gang of Four in October 1976. The then Ministry of Culture, under orders from Jiang Qing, prohibited performances of Peking Opera plays with traditional themes. The actors, actresses, costume and wardrobe people, stage crews, directors . . . all those involved in its production . . . were severely criticized, made to do manual work in the rural areas of China and even imprisoned. In the place of traditional theatre, performances of eight model operatic plays based on China's recent revolutionary experiences were offered. During the "cultural revolution" these were almost the sole performances on Chinese stage and cinema. Radio, too, reflected this policy and broadcasts blared out the same lines from the same eight operas year after year. The same was true for TV.

When the Gang of Four was overthrown in 1976, diversity again returned to Chinese life and to the Chinese stage. But there were problems. Many involved in production of Peking Opera had died or grown too old to perform, and it was hard to find talent to take up parts and play them as well as the old masters. But with enormous popular encouragement, the old traditional stories, which are deep in the history and folk-lore of the Chinese people, began to take their place again on a revived stage. A whole host of old favourites of the Peking Opera stage have now returned, and opera schools are teaching a new generation of young actors and actresses. Peking Opera began to appear on radio and TV. Local opera of many kinds began to be staged again all over the country. Peking Opera is back again in its rightful place in Chinese culture.

REWI ALLEY

Autumn 1981

General Lian Po (*The General and the Minister Are Reconciled*)

by Eva Siao

Heavenly King Li with his magic pagoda (*Havoc in Heaven*)   by Eva Siao

A battle scene (*Fighting Ma Chao*)　　　　　　　　　　　　　by Weng Naiqiang

White Snake and her maid Blue Snake (*The White Snake*)   by Eva Siao

Mu Guiying (*left*), standing before the memorial tablet of her husband Commander Yang Zongbao, makes up her mind to resist rather than capitulate. (*Women Generals of the Yang Family*)   **by Weng Naiqiang**

The nymph who falls in love with a mortal (*Giving a Pearl on the Rainbow Bridge*)

by Zhang Zudao

CONTENTS

Cover Picture: Monkey King in *Havoc in Heaven*

Back Cover Picture: The King of Chu in *The King's Parting with His Favourite*

A TRADITIONAL CHINESE ART

醉
酒

The drunken beauty Yang Yuhuan
by Ma De

Beijing is now a great world city, the hub of a vast transportation system that reaches out to many parts of the world. The tourist trade has expanded and now an increasing number of people come in from many lands. Among them are those who want to catch a glimpse of Peking Opera which through all the years of change continues with its age-old forms, simply perfecting them, and remaining high in the affection of the Chinese people. For those who do go to see Peking Opera, this book may be of use in making for a deeper understanding of so powerful an artistic form.

Beijing people who love their opera talk about going to hear an opera, rather than see it. But those who have not yet gained some background of understanding may find it a little difficult at first. If they have been provided with a general outline of the theme of the opera they go to see, it will help them a great deal. Still they will not be able to follow the words, and the high notes in which it is sung may, in the beginning, be too unfamiliar to be fully appreciated. They may return, perhaps, to their hotels saying, "Yes, the costumes were certainly gorgeous, and the battle scenes with those magnificent acrobats — simply terrific!" or those who take a special delight in the human form may say, "The hand and leg movements were most expressive, graceful and artistic." Yet in all this they will have only touched the fringe of the manifold artistry that goes to make up a classical opera performance.

Artistically, Peking Opera is perhaps the most perfect thing of its kind existing in our world today. Its influence is deep in the hearts of the Chinese people, and it is as intensely popular in this living present as it was centuries ago. A knowledge of it is one beginning in the adventure of understanding this quarter of the world's population.

The classical Peking Opera is amazing in that it combines so many forms which, in the Western drama, are separated. It is grand opera, ballet, an acrobatic display and an historical play rolled into one changing and exciting panorama. It definitely sets out to be something different from ordinary life, yet on the other hand it remains intensely human. Its great figures, for instance, are human — its gods, its spirits, its generals and emperors, even its monks and nuns. The fiery old Queen of the Western Heavens, the immortals who drink wine together, hate and love as do the legendary and historical characters whose exploits form so many of the plots. Moral rather than material values predominate: filial piety, love of country, the fidelity of comrades-in-arms find equal place with the love stories common to all peoples at all times. Naturally, the customs and thought are those of the day in which the stories were written, but some very modern conceptions can be found tucked away in the old tales. Today's directors have been very skilful in bringing these to the fore.

Just as folk legend and familiar stories colour so much of the drama of the West, so in China many themes for classical opera are ancient tales that have been handed down until they have become part of the people's thinking. Classical opera may offer many new clues to those who would add to their knowledge and understanding of China and of the Chinese people.

Autumn River   by Ma De

To the sophisticated viewer of plays, Peking Opera may seem at first rather stylized and formal in many of its aspects — though in these times of change, variety is increasing along with all the changes society is undergoing. Yet so rich is the old content that it is only by visiting the theatre very often that a proper appreciation of its subtleties can be gained. Many Chinese people themselves feel this.

In spite of the formalism, however, there is great scope left for the individual actor to carry off a traditional scene in a way that impresses all with his/her genius. The name of Tan Xinpei, the greatest actor in the early 20th century, is better known to the people than are the names of the various warlords who strutted on and off the political stage in those hectic times. His mantle fell on the shoulders of Mei Lanfang, whose name was a household word

Wu·Song drinks deeply before killing a tiger.

by Ma De

all over China. Others such as Zhou Xinfang were as well known in the big cities as was any Hollywood star in America.

The Chinese theatre, with its tradition of selecting the colourful and meaningful from the past, may perhaps be expected in the next great creative age of China to seek new material and new themes. People who do things — make new bridges, climb over mountains, lead vital lives — will in this new age look for these things in operatic themes and music. But the old favourites will not be lost; they are too much a part of the people for that. Themes from the times when Han pioneers threw themselves against terrific obstacles in Central Asia, when the talent and wealth of the world flowed down the Old Silk Road during the Tang dynasty, will continue. Even if they adopt changed forms, they will continue to maintain the hold that the old opera has had on Chinese society in the past.

One can see in the operatic programmes picked for many an evening's entertainment something of this already. It is common for extracts from several operas to be selected — four or five of them — to make up the programme. These dramatic selections show how the interest of the people is increasingly drawn to those human situations which come into most people's lives rather than those which reflect the personal heroism of some very great figure of the past.

There are, of course, many operas as well as many forms of opera. It would require a long, concentrated study to know them all. Further, it is not likely that any visitor to China will become as familiar with Chinese tradition as, for example, the native of Beijing who has been brought up from childhood on stories from the theatre related by his elders. Such a person will naturally be immediately familiar with almost any kind of situation that may develop in any opera. But this need not discourage the visitor, whose best way is to ask and then keep on asking, until one gets into the swing of the thing and the opera begins to exert its fascinating hold.

A few aides and guards symbolize a mighty army on stage.

Practising martial skills
by Di Xianghua

One has only to see a bit of drama — for instance, one of the monkey armies in the court of the Monkey King — to realize that a long and arduous training must have been the lot of the actors before they could present themselves on the stage. Indeed, the training of any operatic star is a painstaking business. Mei Lan-fang, the greatest of the last generation in the theatrical world, came from a family of actors and grew up in the theatre; yet, he had to undergo a very rigorous training indeed. An early start must be made while the actor is still growing, well before adolescence, so as to master the body movements required and ensure the complete co-ordination of mind and muscle. The terrific hand-to-hand fights in some scenes, with all kinds of ancient weapons, in which the actors do not touch each other but nevertheless give the whirlwind effect of a tremendous battle, need a physical and mental precision that can only be acquired by an extremely rigid and careful training. In the old days, it was certainly a hard school in which the teacher was very exacting and far from gentle towards mistakes. Yet it certainly produced some great masters, and there was no lack of recruits who aspired to a stage career.

The lad who came into the theatre in the old days as a pupil-apprentice had a tough life to go through. Training included standing out in the open facing a wall in the early morning practising voice-production; learning how to turn somersaults, how to walk and all the complicated leg and arm movements; learning the various parts. The aspiring actor simply had to succeed in all of them or else spend the rest of his life as an underpaid supernumerary — carrying a banner or acting as a member of the retinue of one of the great lords, if he was lucky enough to hold employment at all. Naturally, both teacher and student were desperately anxious for success, and in the old times the practice of *da xi* — the

Teenagers practising the "water sleeves" technique
with costumes specially designed for classroom use.

by Di Xianghua

rod driving home the lessons — was universal. The lads were pitted against terrific odds at an early age, as were all the child workers of the old society. Underfed and always overworked, most young aspiring actors were handed over to the complete charge of their instructors. Much depended on whether he was humane and liked them or not. Old indentures for apprentices to the theatre used to contain a clause to the effect that no one could interfere with the master's training, even if the boy were beaten to death.

In the Shanghai of the writer's early days, the theatrical world of the International Settlement was controlled by an illiterate gangster, Gu Zhuquan. An actor who once dared to defy him was murdered at a feast table by Gu's gunmen. He paid his way easily out of the small trouble this caused, as he did for subsequent things of the kind.

The great, empty and half-lit theatres of Shanghai smelled stuffy and bad. Nevertheless, they were among the places where the lads of Peking Opera who performed in that huge city did their daily training. The boys always looked tired and poorly nourished. The stage was a struggle for business profit like everything else in that "get-rich-quick" metropolis of those times.

One thinks back on all this as one visits the National School for Peking Opera in Beijing today. No longer does the leering, brute face type of "Gu Laoban" — Master Gu Zhuquan, of Shanghai fame — dominate.

Now the trainees for the stage are no longer a harassed bunch of boys, desperately striving to attain perfection under adverse conditions. The whole school, operated by the People's Government, is bursting with life and vitality. Some four hundred girls and boys there grow up along with the opera simply and naturally. Students begin training for Peking Opera during the middle of their primary-school course at about age ten or eleven. They continue until they have finished high school at around twenty-one. Their practical work is done daily, right alongside their ordinary school subjects, so that theory and practice really run together. Both their class and practical work rooms are spacious and airy, and all students are very evidently kept in top physical condition.

Here musicians for the opera are also trained. Graduates go out to strengthen the many hundreds of Peking Opera troupes that are in such great demand all over the land.

The Peking Opera school also trains boys and girls for local opera, but these trainees come in during the middle of their high-school course, and stay only four years. Their craft does not demand the same perfection as Peking Opera.

In all, the students impress one greatly. Struggle is by no means eliminated, but it is struggle in which the trainee is given every possible assistance to become the victor. The old instructors are people who have come from a life on the stage, and who are keen to hand on their craft.

After a visit, we asked some of the younger trainees to come and

Girls preparing for a dress rehearsal.

by Di Xianghua

be photographed. One of them, the smallest and youngest in the school, himself the son of an actor in Peking Opera, solemnly shook hands and then at our request sang a piece of Peking Opera. Into the song as he sang it, he put much of himself ... his joy of living, his pride of being an actor for the people of the better day.

His notes carried out and over the roofs of the new buildings being constructed, over the green trees bursting with spring leaves. They mingled with the sounds of the resurgent Beijing, of which he was so truly a part. The contrast with the old one had known was so great that, as one listened, suddenly one's eyes felt moist. Once again came the realization of the enormous thing that has happened to the ordinary people of this land.

His song finished, he looked up at his fellow-student, a girl, who was a little older than he. The two of them smiled delightedly at each other.

Specially tiresome in the old days was the training which had to do with learning to play female parts. The female impersonator appeared in the early 18th century when, in the time of the Emperor Qian Long, women were not allowed to appear on the same stage with men. Though the Manchus themselves enjoyed the stage immensely and selected for their own entertainment the best actors, the actors themselves were classed by the official world (along with barbers and prostitutes) as people who could not be allowed to assume court rank. After the fall of the Manchus something of the old tradition still remained, until finally the People's Republic came into being and this was changed.

Boys in partial costume training to portray old men.

by Di Xianghua

The male impersonator must now, as then, learn how to walk naturally and gracefully. The older feminine roles for instance — called *lao dan* parts, in which mothers and aunts, dowager queens and other elderly ladies were impersonated — had always to be done in so slow and dignified a manner that it is said that actors could not consider themselves perfect until they could hold a brush between their knees and walk about without letting it fall. Women's roles of maidservants and the like, wearing gaudy costumes, are called *hua dan*, and women clown parts *cai dan* or *chou dan*.

Among actors there are several well-defined categories in which they move. For instance, the *sheng* are the actors of the chief male roles. This category is subdivided into older men with beards (*lao sheng* or *xu sheng*), young men (*xiao sheng*), the scholar-officials (*wen sheng*), and the army men (*wu sheng*). These last have to be specially trained as their fighting includes much high-grade acrobatic work which demands a very fine degree of co-ordination. The scholar officials (*wen sheng*) have to bring to their roles all the dignity, poise and good manners possible, and the young lads (*xiao sheng*) must sing in a high falsetto to convey an impression of extreme youth.

Next to the *sheng* actors are the *dan* players who perform the women's roles. These too have their subdivisions: the *lao dan* who are the elderly, dignified women; the *qing yi* who are the middle aged and sombrely dressed matrons; and that most exciting of female roles, the *hua dan*, the women who have more acting than singing to do. Then there are the *gui men dan* who represent the innocent young women still kept at home. Then there are the *dao ma dan*, the tough, hard-riding, fighting women like the famous female warrior Hua Mulan or the woman leader of a rebellion.

The *jing* actors play the parts of adventurers, heroes, bandits or other tough-natured people. The *chou* are the clowns; their task is the same as that of the Western clown — to keep the audience laughing and to improvise quips at the right moment to break the tension in some serious play.

Other characters are the *mo* or *fu mo* — a kind of *sheng* but not so imposing; perhaps an old servant or a barbarian general or some other minor character. Then there are the *fu jing* who are minor *jing* characters; these are perhaps not only fierce and tough but also somewhat ridiculous, or at any rate, hardly heroic.

Every actor has to learn an immensely intricate series of body movements; great study is needed to bring these to their high perfection. Leg and foot movements, for instance, deserve a watchful study by the spectator. There are staggering steps, slipping steps, upstairs and downstairs steps, jumping, mincing, side-stepping, cross steps and ghost steps among the many kinds that must be practised and made perfect according to tradition. Graceful action is a first essential coupled with precision. The flexed knee, the high kick, the sweeping exit steps are all highly important. As for the arms, take the long "rippling water" sleeves, for instance. There are over fifty sleeve movements to be learned with these — the sleeve that repulses, that hides what is being said, that disguises the actor, greets or says farewell, calls attention to the character, is used for dusting, weeping or shading the face and, incidentally, for signalling to the orchestra. Hand movements, with the sleeve

Photos by Eva Siao

Xiao sheng (young man)

Wu sheng (military man)

Lao sheng (old man)

20

Qing yi (quiet and gentle female)

Wu dan (woman with martial skills)

Hua dan and *chou dan* (vivacious young woman and female clown)

Lao dan (old woman)

Jing (painted face)

Jing (painted face — the red flower signifies a dissolute character.)

Chou (clown)

Wu sheng (a minor military role)

Long tao (aides or guards of a commander or official)

Sun Yujiao doing her needlework with an invisible thread. (*The Jade Bracelet*)
Photos by Eva Siao

thrown back, are even more intricate. They may show the helplessness of an unprotected woman, the clenched fist of fighting, or disapproval, or yielding. There are special hand gestures for swimming, for pointing (which is very difficult to do correctly in different situations — anger, hate, friendship or whatever it might be), besides the movement needed for pointing with a fan.

There are also complicated movements to be mastered in dealing with the great pheasant feathers worn on the head of military commanders, enemy generals, and tribesmen, which are used to display anger, determination or other emotions. Waist movements are also traditional and well studied. These have been all reduced to a science by generations of teachers, who have done their best to analyse every emotion and find appropriate gestures for expressing it. There is even a list of the twenty kinds of laughing and smiling, all of which have to be rehearsed and practised to perfection.

Gestures are used for opening doors — a character enters a room by stepping high over an imaginary threshold. Mounting and dismounting from an imaginary charger is done with considerable flourish and effect by taking or giving to an attendant a tasselled riding whip. All have to be done in strict accordance with tradition. The resulting poise, and astonishing control over every muscle, is something that may be reached in Peking Opera, but perhaps hardly anywhere else in the world.

Such things as seating a guest or taking one's own seat are done precisely in line with tradition. The manner does not vary. Opening doors or closing windows include actions which show unmistakably what the actor is doing; of course, opening and closing from inside and from outside are different.

There are some stage actions that will, perhaps, puzzle the foreign onlooker at first. But by dint of patient enquiry one will find the answer to them all. Some actions, for example, have their origins in court manners of bygone days. Drinking wine, for instance, with the wide sleeve of the other hand shielding the face; this was considered a polite thing to do in the old imperial court ... long beards sometimes not being very convenient in wine drinking. A male actor may laugh openly on the stage, but it is far more usual for a woman to conceal her laughter with her long sleeve.

An actor holding a hand up between the other actors and himself, while he speaks to himself and the audience, precludes the other characters on the stage from hearing anything whatsoever of what is being said. Standing erect and tense against the outside of a building or building support shows that the actor is either listening in, or else escaping notice. The movements needed in going up and down stairs are easy to follow — the lady picks up her skirt with one hand, while the man whirls one of his long sleeves around his right arm leaving his hand free to pick up his gown. Sewing is shown with deliberate and technically exact movements, despite the complete absence of either thread or needle. Though the way things are to be shown has been set by tradition,

Mu Guiying fights off an invader from the Western Xia. (*Women Generals of the Yang Family*)

by Weng Naiqiang

yet each actor can give his or her own interpretation. One thinks of the ability with which some actors show the very old woman coming on to the stage ... gripping her staff with determination, though her feet drag with age. Both the weakness and the strength are demonstrated, just as they are with the blustering general, magnificently arrayed, feet lifted high and legs wide apart. He glories in all his military manhood, yet through it all shows some of the weaknesses of stupidity and conceit that lead to his defeat.

There are many, many other actor conventions, which the theatre-goer will soon learn to appreciate. A woman, for instance, conceals her thumb always, while a great "painted-face" hero will make much of his. Different characters mount or dismount a horse do it in different ways. Usually, only the martial heroines ride; the others go in carriages. A woman picking up an object from the stage floor makes the whole movement a rhythmical one by bending gracefully over to one side and carefully balancing herself with one arm outstretched, lest she fall on her small feet.

Because the essence of the Peking Opera is its operatic content, an actor must sing quite well to be considered in the first rank. It will take the foreign observer some time to distinguish the values Beijing audiences p'ace on various pieces of song; but after listening carefully, one will begin to appreciate the differences in rendering and begin to wonder why this was not evident in the first place.

COSTUMES

Magnificent embroideries and combinations of colour of the costumes will at first so bedazzle the newcomer to the opera that he will find the spectacle enough in itself, without wondering what meaning the dress conveys. Some of the present operatic clothing has a resemblance to that of the Ming period (1368-1644 A.D.) when the official world itself did actually indulge in very splendid robes of great extravagance, though actually operatic costuming is really a mixture of different styles of succeeding dynasties with all kinds of exaggerations and additions. The Confucian tradition (with its strong emphasis on rules of conduct for gentle people rather than on comfort, health or preference of the masses) preferred every possible part of the person to be well covered from the light of the sun; hence the long sleeves which have to be tossed back to reveal the exquisite hand movements, hence the swirling robes. The gorgeous headdresses, the jewelled girdles of the men and the hair ornaments of the women, the magnificent embroideries and the great, high court shoes which increase the height and majesty of the more important figures all give great scope to the theatrical costume designer.

Major military heroes as well as the minor ones wear a kind of padded armour called *kao*, which are emblazoned with many ornaments. Courtiers wear dragon robes called *mang*, the lower borders of which are embroidered to represent waves. The colours of such robes give some indication of the status of the character portrayed — yellow for the imperial family; red for the high nobility; white for old officials, civilian or military; red or blue for upright men; and black for people of somewhat violent character. The official gown, called *guan yi*, is like the *mang*. It has embroidered squares on back and front with different colours denoting different grades of officialdom.

There are appropriate costumes for every character, each with its name. The blue-lined coat called the *tie ze* denotes the student, a cream-coloured one similar to the *tie ze* is worn by an aged villager, and so on.

An emperor wears a hat of pearls with tassels hanging down at both sides. Sometimes leaders of people's rebellions wear similar hats. The long pheasant-tail plumes and the fox-tails attached to

A painted face

◁ Xiangyu, the King of Chu (*The King's Parting with His Favourite*)
by Weng Naiqiang

Painting the face: from start to finish

the headdresses of warriors often indicate that they belong to the pastoral or hill-dwelling enemies of the ancient Middle Kingdom. When a warrior engages his foe he throws the fox-tails back over his shoulders; the pheasant plumes are seized with a huge flourish to indicate that the wearer is about to advance.

Moustaches and beards also have special significance. The beard divided into three indicates the righteousness and integrity of the wearer. A short moustache shows that the wearer is somewhat crude and rough, and those which sweep upwards belong to tricky, slippery fellows.

Perhaps the most fascinating study in connection with stage costume is that of the painted faces of the actors. Masks are worn usually only when animals are represented — tiger, wolf, pig, bear and so on. The art of painting the face, however, has been very highly developed; and each painted face has a special meaning to the knowledgeable theatre-goer.

The more admirable characters are usually painted in relatively simple colours. Enemy leaders of martial characters . . . toughs, bandits, hardened soldiers, rebels . . . have more complicated designs on their faces. A lot of red indicates courage, loyalty, straightforwardness; more black denotes impulsiveness. A blue face is a cruel one. A crook who is completely untrustworthy is given a white, often twisted face. Many characters are known instantly

by their make-up, such as Cao Cao of the State of Wei, in "The Three Kingdoms" (220-280 A.D.) story; or Guan Gong of Shu in the same period, who was later deified in almost all parts of China. The experienced theatre-goer recognizes such people by their faces as soon as they come on the stage. Being well-acquainted with the story allows one to relax and pay full attention to the niceties of the presentation.

There are other characters which are instantly recognizable — the *chou* or clowns. Women comedians are called *chou dan*, and army clowns *wu chou*. Clowns have a very privileged place on the Chinese operatic stage; they represent the common people. Popular story says that the "Brilliant Emperor" of the Tang dynasty would sometimes play these parts himself in his imperial "Pear Garden Troupe of Drama", a private one attached to the imperial household taking its name from that portion of the palace where the emperor himself at times directed the instruction of selected young people. Clowns are usually known by their white-painted noses, which often have a sort of butterfly or other shape painted across them, and their eyes made into oblong boxes.

Among the *jing* roles — heroes, adventurers, bandits and other kinds of tough-natured people — the better of them have plainly-painted faces. The more involved characters show all sorts of combinations of colours and line, some of which are based on ancient sculpture or traditional paintings, and some on pure fancy. The triangu'ar eye is considered rather crafty. Here again, colours depict character in accordance with custom — red, good; white, bad; black, brusque; blue, cruel, and so on.

Other devices that the actor uses to accentuate features or figure are much the same as those used in all theatre work — except perhaps that of making the eyes seem bigger. Here, the forehead is bound tightly back with a string of horsehair and a cap of black gauze is pulled over the head. Some of the actors not only wear the high court shoes that make them appear exceptionally tall, but under their robes they also wear a thick padded-cotton jacket, called a *bang ao,* which adds to stoutness.

In the past stage effects and props were not much thought about, all eyes being for the actors themse'ves. The heap of props from which the stage hands would select the appropriate item in what to the Westerner then seemed a completely casual manner, used to

A battle scene (*Women Generals of the Yang Family*)

be in full view of the audience. In those days the attendants would move around among the actors, pouring tea, arranging chairs, setting disarranged costumes to rights or assisting the wounded and killed to get off the stage in battle scenes. These somewhat distracting features of old times have today disappeared, but the old-style props and simple stage furniture are still being used in many cases. Reliance is on traditional gesture and mime instead of the more elaborate scenic effects, though these, too, are now being experimented with. Riding in a cart or a chariot, for example, is made perfectly plain by two flags with wheels painted on them. These are held by an attendant, on either side of a lady who is proceeding by this means of locomotion. An oar, wielded by a typical boatman, is sufficient to give a very complete idea of travel by boat. The way the boatman helps his passenger on to his rocking craft is a marvel of make-believe. Complete invisibility is reached when an actor mounts a table or chair. A man escaping

by Weng Naiqiang

Costuming: from start to finish

from an enemy will run across the stage, lifting his feet high, then, crouching on a chair and covering his face with his hands, he will be understood to have sought refuge in some high place. No matter how the enemy dash around him, they cannot find him.

A strip of painted cloth held up between two poles can serve as a gateway for an official entrance or exit. The long overgown thrown off shows that the warrior is ready for battle. Perhaps the only bit of real scenery on the old stage was the city wall, painted bricks on canvas which was brought on the stage by two attendants.

The duster of horsehair waved across the stage may indicate the presence of a ghost, a god, a fairy, a eunuch, a forest monk or a hermit; the tossing about of some burning substance that devils are around.

A dead man, if he has to remain on the stage for the purposes of the action, has a dark cloth over his face. Others who are killed in fighting, for example, either roll off the stage or get up after they have fallen down, and run off. Some round object wrapped in a red cloth is the head of an executed person. An actor jumping down from a chair is drowning himself in a well or a river. A ghost has bits of white paper stuck around his ears. When night comes, a candle or a lamp (unlighted) will be brought in, or else the orchestra indicates it by sounding the night watches on drum, gong or other instrument.

In olden times generals sent their orders with an arrow, the idea being to indicate that the message must be taken quickly and that it was authentic. On the stage a big arrow, often very ornate, is used. Imperial commands are always written on an oblong yel-low strip, sometimes of silk, bearing the two characters *sheng zhi* — by the divine command.

All these and many other traditional devices are well known to the theatre-goer. A sick man wears a long strip of yellow silk around his head with the ends hanging down his back. Each soldier carrying a flag represents many men — one or two thousand, prob-

Photos by Eva Siao

ably. An arrested person usually has a long chain round his neck, which hangs down in front.

To show weather conditions, a flag with black lines drawn across it indicates a storm; a flag with the character for "water" means there is a flood. Rain is easy to distinguish: one sees the actors carrying umbrellas or dodging pools of water. Tossing up of tiny bits of paper gives the idea of snowing.

The placing of the scanty stage furniture is very important. The main stage props are a table and two chairs; often this is all. There are all kinds of rules about the exact position of the chairs for different characters — behind the table, in front of it, daughter sitting to the right of parents, son to the left, and so on. Sometimes two chairs together may represent a bed. Official standards, big round sunshades and long-handled fans, are carried on to show the retinue of a great personage or an emperor, either of earth or of heaven. Many lanterns are important when the action takes place at night. Officials reporting to the emperor hold in their hands a curved piece of ivory called *hu* — a mark of respect reflecting a real practice coming down from antiquity when jade or stone was used for this purpose.

Sometimes a line of men enters with placards on which clouds are painted. These are carried in front of them to represent this phenomenon. At other times a long cloth is tossed up and down to show the motion of waves. But devices like this are easy to recognize; the theatre-goer will understand them when he sees them without any explanation.

If the foreign visitor has taken the precaution of getting a clear outline of the story first, many other details will be apparent also. For instance, the escape of two women firewood cutters from a jail into which they had been unjustly cast is portrayed very clearly: one of them carefully helps the other up one chair, then over its back and down another.

On terms used to denote various kinds of music that have been used in Chinese opera, one notes that *xi pi* or Shaanxi tune was one of the first. It is an old term whose derivation is lost in antiquity, but which became popular all over China certainly by Ming dynasty times. *Er huang* is a name taken from the places of Huanggang and Huangpi in Hubei and means the style of the "Two Huangs". It is a style less strident than that called *xi pi*.

In the style called *bang zi* the time is well marked by the use of two bits of wood, one round and the other flat on one side and rounded on the other, which are struck together. Provincial opera is sometimes called *bang zi* as is that of Hebei and Henan.

Then there are the *kun qu* styles of music, probably very old styles which were brought back to popularity in the late Ming period by some dramatic enthusiasts in and around Kunshan, a city in Jiangsu Province not far from Shanghai. *Kun qu* reflects the Yiyang tunes of Jiangxi and the Haiyen tunes of Zhejiang as well as some other folk music.

To the newcomer the orchestra, which seems to the Western visitor to have a superabundance of gongs, cymbals and drums, may appear somewhat harsh. Yet it will be found that it suits the high notes of the operatic song very well, and one soon comes to appreciate it and to feel that it is no longer strange. The accompaniment for the voice is played on the *jing hu* — the two-stringed fiddle named after the Hu or tribesmen from north of the Great Wall from whom the instrument first came. Flutes are also used, the bamboo kind, held parallel to the face when played. The *sheng* or reed flute is really a small organ and has chords. Then there are moon guitars and three-stringed guitars which came from the western tribesmen of the steppe. Big and small drums, a bell, cymbals and the *ban* or wooden time-beater which does for the orchestra what the conductor does for his musicians in a Western performance, round out the orchestra.

Some of the great actors are inseparable from their *jing hu* accompanists, with whom they work very much as a team. Entrances and exits have a musical accompaniment. An actor, before breaking into song, will speak his last words in a certain way so that the orchestra knows the song is about to begin. In the middle of a song the *jing hu* accompanist plays a few bars — called *guo men* (getting past the door) — to give the singer a rest.

The entrances of the great are always heralded by a great burst of cymbal and drums, a bit of procedure which possibly has something to do with the impact of Kitans, Nuchens, Mongols and Manchus during the past thousand years, and their absorption into north China where Peking Opera has its home.

In past times the orchestra sat on the stage exposed to the full view of the audience, but it is now generally concealed in the wings.

Peking Opera orchestra: the conductor sits in the middle with the principal fiddle to his left. by Hang Hai

SOME
NOTES
ON
ORIGINS

From the earliest recorded times the Chinese people, like all others, have expressed themselves in song and dance, from the magical fertility dances to those that expressed their hope for a good harvest or their joy in the result of their toil. Dance and song very early became a part of court ritual. We know that in Zhou times they were considered things that every child should learn. State music was composed for emperors, to which dancers moved holding in their hands various ritual ornaments. Blind people were trained as musicians and, because of this, had an honoured place in the society of that day.

Some promotion of opera from the song and dance of early times seems to have taken place in the imperial courts where rulers demanded amusement from acrobats, jesters and story-tellers. But the dramatic expression of course came from the people as their own creation. Music, narrative and dance began to be integrated into the precursor of opera as we have it today. Historical incidents, especially those which caught a popular trend of thought, naturally became favourite themes. Chinese poetry, always composed to be sung or chanted, could be used freely in such an entertainment.

Practically every dynasty has left some record of the state of the drama in its day, if only of that which was confined to the court. We know too that when the great merchants' and craftsmen's guilds spread over the country they carried stages with them for the production of plays. In an early account of the workers' life in Jingdezhen, the great pottery centre in Jiangxi, it is noted that the kiln managers were to be fined for not keeping their agreement to pay for the staging of operas for the workers on a stipulated number of days in the year. There are many country places, especially along the "Old Silk Road" in the northwest, where it can still be seen that almost every ancient temple had a stage opposite its gate where drama in its operatic form was sung on people's festivals in bygone times.

◁ Coloured paper-cuts on pages 34 through 41 from Weixian County, Shandong Province

The Yuan period (1279-1368) is considered the golden age of the classical opera, though in various forms it dates back as far as the Zhou. In Western Han times the "hundred plays" (*bai xi*) were a very popular, largely acrobatic form of people's drama which spread over the whole land. But it was in the Yuan period — the Mongol dynasty of which Kublai Khan was the first emperor — that the opera underwent certain changes. By then north China had already had a period of overlordship by the Jin and Liao tribesmen who had begun to be absorbed as Chinese. The Mongols conquered both the Jin empire and that of the Southern Song with its beautiful capital at Hangzhou in Zhejiang and ousted the old ruling bureaucracy. No longer did the examination system carry the poor but brilliant student into high office. So among the intellectuals there was a great striving for self-expression. At the same time, the foreign superstructure itself began to be absorbed. Though the Yuan drama was an evolution of that of Song which had preceded it, there were innovations in line with the new integration of peoples. The great hero with a huge voice shouting his defiant song began to replace earlier forms in which there were choruses of sweeter and more rhythmic voices.

It was in the Yuan period that many of the stories handed down by oral tradition, which were later incorporated into such popular novels as *The Three Kingdoms* and the *Outlaws of the Marsh* and others, began to be used as themes for the opera. They could be played because they placed the desire for change in a historical setting and were woven around legendary or historical happenings from that part of Chinese history (in the case of the Three Kingdoms) that came after the end of the Han dynasty. *The Three Kingdoms* is set in the 3rd century A.D., when China was divided into three kingdoms, each struggling for ascendancy over the other. The story of the struggles between these three, with its plot and counterplot, has so captured the imagination of succeeding generations of people that today almost everyone knows something of these tales.

Outlaws of the Marsh is a very long story, telling of what was actually a peasant revolt against the bureaucracy and decadence of the Northern Song dynasty. The heroes, all of whom are people who have offended the government in some way, collect together gradually in one band under Song Jiang in the Liangshan Hills. From here they sally forth in the manner of Robin Hood to relieve the distressed. Before their final defeat they succeed in bringing together armies of considerable proportions which acutely tax the strength of the Northern Song dynasty. Among the many vivid tales told of this band of brothers are stories of success, of treason and betrayal, of intense loyalty and devotion to their fighting group. Among the most lovable characters is the rash Black Li Kui, who makes many mistakes because of his impulsiveness; but who nevertheless is warm of heart.

There was a very widespread use of drama in the Song periods when the official plays were known as *guan ben* and the ones in private homes as *yuan ben*. After the Song dynasty was driven south of the Changjiang (Yangtze River), considerable development took place around Wenzhou in east Zhejiang. There, Gao Zecheng wrote the *Tale of the Lute* (*Pi Pa Ji*) which has been a famous opera ever since it was produced in 1347 during the Yuan dynasty.

In the Ming period (1368-1644) some very fine operatic music was created, much of it based on earlier forms. The *kun qu* form of opera came into great favour and the music of Huizhou, a lovely old city in southern Anhui Province, became popular, as did that of Yiyang in Jiangxi.

With the coming of the Manchu (Qing) dynasty in 1644, many dramatic writers, especially Hong Sheng, tried to express in their works some of the feelings of the people. Hong Sheng used stories of an ancient period — that of the Tang dynasty — to illustrate his criticism of the present, and he was in consequence persecuted. His work is strongly appreciated even today: he was commemorated in the new Beijing in 1954, on the 200th anniversary of his death.

An English translation of his opera, *The Palace of Eternal Youth* (*Chang Sheng Dian*), was made in 1955 and should be read with the understanding that the real purpose of the plot is to denounce those traitors who turned to serve what was at that time a foreign regime.

> *Yet those rotten courtiers, those good-for-nothing curs,*
> *Who talked so much of loyalty and piety,*
> *As soon as disaster came just turned their coats*
> *To grab at wealth and position.*
> *They fawn and cringe when they accept new titles,*
> *Taking their deadly foe as their benefactor.*
> *Have they no sense of shame?**

Though the setting is in the Tang dynasty and the protest is against other foreign conquerors, this must have hit home. This opera, though political in intent, also appeals to the human side, for all people are interested in love stories. Here is the prologue to the play:

> *Since ancient times how few lovers*
> *Have really remained constant to the end;*
> *But those who were true have come together at last,*
> *Even though thousands of miles apart,*
> *Even though torn from each other by death. And all*
> *Who curse their unhappy fate are simply those*
> *Lacking in love. True love moves heaven and earth,*
> *Metal and stone, shines like the sun and lights*
> *The pages of old histories....*

It is no wonder that the Manchu rulers did their best to stamp out the kind of opera where strong opposition to feudal rule or

---

* Hong Sheng, *The Palace of Eternal Youth*, p. 171, Foreign Languages Press, Beijing.

sentiments of national feeling were expressed. Moreover, they set up a commission in Yangzhou, northern Jiangsu Province, where many rich merchants and others lived who patronized the disliked forms of opera. The duty of this commission was to delete from the old opera the offending passages and bring it into line, in form and content, with the type the Manchu overlords approved of. This was in 1777 during the Qian Long period; and the result of this action was that in the end many popular operas which had had great influence with the people were either revised, banned or completely lost.

At the time of the revolution against the Manchus, 1911-1912, many members of the imperial household, who till then had been amateurs, went on the stage as professionals. The onslaught of Western imperialism made the patriotic operas more and more popular and in time they began to be used as an interpretation of the wishes and feelings of the people.

So it is interesting to see how the Yuan drama, the basis for most of the modern Peking Opera, was an expression of popular feeling by the Chinese people in a time of foreign domination. It flowered again at the time of the domination of the Manchus and afterwards during the period of foreign imperialist control. At all these periods, the bringing back of the stories of old, with their struggles and their heroes, their brilliance and their patriotism, brought hope to the people.

The first Chinese opera ever to come to the West was the one called *Search for and Rescue of the Orphan* written by a Yuan playwright Ji Junxiang who lived somewhere about the middle of the 14th century. Since it is not easy to sing, it is not performed much in China today. Set in the Spring and Autumn Period of the Zhou dynasty the story is about a civil war, in which a military leader tries to kill all the members of the ruling house but misses one child who is saved by a loyal servant. It was called *The Zhao Family Orphan* in the West and no less than five adaptations of it were made. In England the play was converted into a political one attacking the corrupt Walpole government; it departed widely from its original. Hatchett, the English playwright who adapted it, makes one of his characters say:

> *Are we not likewise prey'd upon like carrion,*
> *By locust place-men and by martial drones?*
> *Are we not up to th' chin in debts and taxes?*
> *Trick'd where we trust and hated where we love?*
> *By foe and by ally, alike despis'd?*
> *Are we not drain'd by ev'ry state cathartick,*
> *By costly peaces and expensive wars?*

A French version in which Voltaire propounded his ideas of the triumph of reason also existed, and it is said by a biographer that Goethe also based his play *Elpenor* on *The Zhao Family Orphan*.

The role of the classical Chinese opera in sustaining the morale of the common people during the terrible century before liberation is certainly very considerable. The chief figures are beings from another world, from the ancient periods of China's history. But it is a world which the people loved to enter because it recalled the heroic struggles of the past. The common man, seeing the ancient heroes fighting mightily to overthrow foreign rule, would say to himself: "Soon we shall do it again!" He would see and admire the righteous Judge Bao, who never failed to find the absolute truth in every case — so different from the justice which the people then met in daily life. He would see quick swords raised in defence of righteous causes, and great, pompous officials topple down before the brothers of Liangshan or Sun, the Monkey King.

The Monkey is truly a popular hero, for nothing is too big or too pompous for him to take on — not even the whole court of heaven, the Pearly Emperor included. Some of his exploits are familiar to readers of English in Arthur Waley's *Monkey*, a selection of episodes from the novel *Journey to the West* (*Xi You Ji*), a full translation of which is being published by the Foreign Languages Press. The book, an old classic in China, is a parody on the Tang dynasty account of Xuan Zhuang's long journey to India in search of the Buddhist scriptures. The Monkey is a very resourceful character, a puller-down of anything he feels like pulling down. Many episodes from the story have been dramatized in the opera, and Monkey's antics are a never-ending source of delight to audiences. In the minds of the Chinese people he has always represented the common man, scoring some of the victories which the people would like to score, against all the forces that were arrayed against him.

From the time China's Red Army was organized, and through the formation of a series of resistance bases, the problem of education of the people and the army itself was naturally a great one. As small drama groups grew into bigger ones and as technique was perfected and folk music adapted, so did the revolutionary theatre develop.

An entirely new form of opera arose. This evolved in a series of stages during the fight against Japan, in the liberated areas of the country, in the War of Liberation that followed the Japanese defeat. It was spread mainly by the drama groups of the People's Liberation Army and it told stories of the everyday life of the people and their struggles in an absolutely electrifying way. The performances in thousands of towns and villages by the army drama groups in the period immediately following liberation opened the eyes of the people in a way nothing else could have done. They saw their own struggles enacted before their eyes; all the bitterness caused by the landlords and their armies was there in living reality. They saw that change had come and that power was really in their hands. In form, this new type of opera was something closer to those more familiar to the rest of the world, though the music was based on folk songs and the instruments used were often classical Chinese instruments. It too played to crowded houses whenever it was brought to the stage. It had a deep real-

ism which people recognized as their own experience and a philosophy which was right down to earth.

Although these new liberation operas will live long and will be accorded an honoured position in the permanent operatic tradition of China, they have in no way taken, or ever would seem likely to take, the place of the classical Peking Opera. The two are entirely different.

Peking Opera has a lasting fascination and a definite and expanding role to play in the mighty new land that has so swiftly and so brilliantly emerged from the ruins of the old. Many of the operatic plots, with little or no adaptation, still have that ageless freshness of appeal to the people. Naturally, the actors, in line with their new political understanding and as people's artists, place a new emphasis on some of the parts played.

One old and very popular opera still currently being played in Beijing, for example, is *Iron Faced and Unselfish*, the story of an event around a flood disaster in the Song dynasty. All the officials concerned — magistrate, prefect, imperial commissioner — are grasping and corrupt and share the extra levies for flood relief among themselves, instead of using them for the people. But at court there is the righteous judge, Bao Gong, who works for justice. With the help of the emperor's uncle he foils their greedy plans and sets the situation right. Many people who see this opera must recall personal experiences of the great floods of past days, such as the disasters of 1931 when corrupt officials and traders of that day rushed to the scene to use their power to gain profit from the situation. They must rejoice when they see this ancient drama, knowing that now corruption has gone for good and their country is united in one whole to fight and guard against whatever natural disaster may come.

Another successful recent presentation is a story from *Outlaws of the Marsh* which tells of the killing of a tiger by some hunters. The tiger in its death struggle falls from the mountainside and lands in the grounds of a rich landlord, whose men seize it and carry it off to collect the reward which has been offered. When the hunters arrive at the landlord's home to demand the rightful spoils of their chase, the landlord falsely accuses them of being bandits and attempting armed assault on him. It is worthwhile having a good seat for a performance of this kind for the actors, especially when they are facing such scenes as those depicting torture and imprisonment at the hands of the corrupt magistrate and the landlord, play their part with a tremendously realistic brilliance and strength, shown so well in their facial expressions.

Today, whether it be the White Snake, the heroine Hua Mulan, the tribal princess Mu Guiying, or the brave fisherman and his beautiful daughter who took revenge for the wrongs perpetrated against them, the old stories are taking on a new richness. They become part of the new life of a people who have themselves struggled against aggression and have given birth to countless new heroes and heroines, worthy inheritors of the glories of past struggles.

These old stories too are a natural background for the newer heroic ones that come from the great events of today — the conservancy projects on the Huai and Yellow rivers, the Wuhan cities defending themselves against flood, the vast endeavours of industrialization and continued resistance against aggression.

More and more new drama will be written and will become part of that vast store which is the Chinese people's heritage. Already stories of the Taipings, the revolutionary peasants of the 19th century, of the tragic life of Qu Yuan, the great poet of the 4th century B.C., have been made into impressive operas. In November 1955 they commemorated in Guangzhou the actor Li Wenmao who had died a hero's death just one hundred years before. He had a group of players to fight alongside the peasants of the Taiping revolution against Manchu imperial oppression.

How many people see the opera every day? Surely more than ten million of them! Local operas exist in a tremendous variety of forms, but the form and influence of the Peking Opera has penetrated every corner of the land and adds to the delight and sets standards for the opera everywhere. The great dramatic festivals which have been held in Beijing and other places have brought to light a store of talent that has hitherto gone unregarded. Actors now take their rightful places as truly national figures, loved and admired by the millions who are cheered and inspired by their art.

Before leaving this brief introduction to a very great Chinese institution, a little more might be said on what steps are being taken to see that all which has been evolved so carefully through the generations is not lost. Today there are many training centres for young actors and actresses, and one remembers well going to a performance where the performers were all students of ages from ten to twenty. They played very well indeed, but one could better appreciate the immense perfection of the popular actors on the adult stage when one watched the portrayal of these talented beginners. They could not quite co-ordinate the completely motionless outstretched hand with intricate leg movements ... not quite attain the magnificent poise and complete control over each bodily action of the finished actor.

In this demonstration of learners was all the life and freshness that only youngsters can give. It was another proof, if any proof is needed, that most Chinese are born actors, for they so evidently loved and lived the parts they were playing.

After attending this performance, it was good to go and see at one of the bigger Beijing theatres a presentation made by graduate student actors of the National School of Peking Opera. The ladies came on with a polish and professional charming glide while the great generals entered with a most convincing and terrific swagger, their back flags fluttering and the bright red pompon on their headdresses all a-quivering. Especially good was the much-loved scene of Sun, the Monkey King, defeating the cohorts of Heaven. The whole act was a breathless storm of dance and acrobatics with the old folktale running through, brought out in a clear and delightful

manner. There is certainly a rising generation of actors coming on to fill the places of their elders, who will do credit to them.

The tradition of training for opera in China is a very ancient one. For instance, in the 8th century A D after the capital at Chang'an in the Tang dynasty had been sacked and the existing court driven away, the great Tang poet Du Fu wrote longingly from Kweifu in Sichuan. After listening to a southern revival of old opera in which some of the players were trained in the old Chang'an, he thought back on the magnificence of the other day. A translation of his lines is as follows:

> *Where the strain from stringed instruments*
> *stirs the hearts of older officials; where*
> *the beauties of the scene are enough to sway*
> *even spirits or immortals; now in this southern court*
> *songs of Kai Yuan times are sung by pupils*
> *of the Pear Garden; and as they sing,*
> *the sweetness of their song spreads through*
> *the palace, tears flow from eyes, and lips*
> *move in symphony.*

Now, all the bigger industrial centres that are coming into being have permanent Peking Opera companies playing in the theatres that have been erected among the new homes of the working people there. Indeed, one can see the revived Peking Opera all over China today. In its new form, it is a theatre superbly costumed and magnificently played, resting on the most solid base of all, that of the love and appreciation of the people. Its organization runs parallel and interlinks with other people's organizations in the collective way that all such operate in. The genius of the Chinese people is their ability to work in the group, and the new order now gives additional responsibility and strength to all such that operate for the common good.

In China today there is not only the great work which is being carried out in the training of new actors for the people, but also there is painstaking and widespread research being done into the whole operatic tradition of the country. Wherever survivals of old forms are found, they are closely investigated, and especially in the realm of music where much is being discovered and preserved for all time. The old musical instruments and the melodies played on them become familiar again.

In consequence of all of this, it may be safely said that the creative side of future operatic development will be in line with the best Chinese tradition. Surely there will be change, for with industrialization the people change. For instance, there is now the demand that more scenery be used and that this be of the highest quality. This need is one that is being experimented with very successfully in some of the new productions now being staged.

In conclusion one may say that the people of China today, although they warmly receive the diversity of theatre that is developing, will certainly not forget their first love, the Peking Opera.

SYNOPSES OF FIFTEEN PLAYS

HAVOC
IN
HEAVEN

Havoc in Heaven is based on one of the stories in the 16th-century fantasy novel *Journey to the West*. Its hero is the ever-popular folk hero, the cheerful and disrespectful Monkey King.

His name is Sun Wukong, and he rather feels that he has been slighted by being given an impressive title in Heaven but no real duties. Then, because of not being invited to a feast given by the Heavenly Queen Mother, he starts out on an escapade of insubordination. He eats the sacred peaches and other rare delicacies and drinks the celestial wine, all of which had been reserved for the Queen Mother's guests of gods and fairies. He continues by swallowing the most precious elixir of life, and then finally retreats back to his cave-dwelling on the Mountain of Flowers and Fruit.

There follows a great stir in the court of Heaven. The Jade Emperor orders all the important heavenly generals to lead their mighty armies to capture the mischievous Monkey. But he uses his tremendous magic power to frustrate Heaven's attempts to crush him.

Havoc in Heaven is a rollicking tale which Peking Opera does full justice to. The Monkey King's magic wand throws back the swords of almost any number of enemy soldiers. His somersaults and intricate steps entrance the audience, while his complete effrontery ever reduces them to mirth.

An envoy (*kneeling*) dispatched by the Emperor of Heaven feigns respect to tempt Monkey to accept an official post in Heaven.

Left:
Feeling slighted, he proceeds to wreak havoc at the banquet by helping himself to a pitcher of celestial wine.

Right:
He also finishes off a flask of precious Golden Elixir Pills.

Monkey learns from the fairies that he has not been invited to the Peach Banquet.

Heavenly King Li (*holding magic pagoda*) seeks the aid of the Four Great Heavenly Kings to capture the Monkey King.

Fierce fighting ensues

All photos of **Havoc in Heaven** by Weng Naiqiang

Lady Zhaojun is sent to marry a tribal chieftain far beyond the frontier.

LADY ZHAOJUN CROSSING THE FRONTIER

This opera, adapted from a romance entitled *Tale of the Tomb,* describes how Wang Zhaojun, a beautiful lady from the court of Emperor Yuandi of the Western Han dynasty (206 B.C.-23 A.D.), was forcibly sent to marry a chieftain of the Huns (a minority people living beyond the Great Wall) for the purpose of ensuring peace between the two peoples. It depicts what she saw and felt on the journey.

Having bid farewell to civil and military officials, Wang Zhaojun steps onto a carriage accompanied by Prince Wang Long, the emperor's younger brother, and leaves Chang'an, the capital, with extreme reluctance.

Before long, the carriage arrives at Yanmen, a pass on the frontier. The mountain road is so rugged that Wang Zhaojun, helped by a groom, has to mount a horse. The biting wind and the bizarre scenes of mysterious fog and scurrying clouds arouse nostalgia. Sitting in the saddle, she begins to play the lute and sing of her love for her native country. In this mood she reaches Fenguan Pass, whose exotic scenery again makes her long to return to her hometown and her parents. But on reflection, she realizes that she is now near the frontier and it would be hopeless to turn back. Instead, she sadly continues on her journey.

Lady Zhaojun rides on the back of a horse led by her bold cavalier.

Photos by Eva Siao

THE
JADE
BRACELET

Widow Sun has a young and beautiful daughter named Yujiao. Both mother and daughter raise chickens as a means of subsistence. One day while her mother is away from home, Yujiao sits at the doorway doing some needlework. A young man, Fu Peng, comes by and approaches her on the pretext of buying chickens. The two fall in love at first sight, but both are so embarrassed that they do not know how to express their love.

As he leaves, Fu Peng purposely drops a jade bracelet as token of his love. Overflowing with the happiness of her first love but not wanting anyone else to know of it, Yujiao picks up the bracelet discreetly. But she is seen by the woman living next door, who good-humouredly teases her about the bracelet. Being of a mild and bashful disposition, Yujiao cannot conceal the fact and finally admits her love. The warm-hearted neighbour obtains an embroidered handkerchief from Yujiao and sends it to Fu as a return gift in order to show the young woman's love for him.

Traditional Peking Opera mime, such as the opening of the chicken coop, the feeding of the chickens and the use of the needle and thread in embroidery work reflect the everyday life of the characters in the opera.

Yujiao and Fu Peng fall in love at first sight.

Yujiao is teased by her good-hearted neighbour.

Yujiao rejoices in the discovery of a bracelet left behind by Fu Peng.

Photos by Weng Naiqiang

THE CROSSROADS

This is a rollicking, joyous piece of drama, based on an ancient Chinese folktale.

An upright and brave general, Jiao Zan, has been unjustly convicted and sentenced to exile. His commander is not convinced on his guilt and orders a young officer, Ren Tanghui, to secretly follow and protect him.

Arriving at an inn situated at the junction of three roads, Jiao and his rascally guards are received by the innkeeper, a kind-hearted and jovial fellow who finds the convict an honest and just man.

Overhearing the guards plotting to murder Jiao, the innkeeper and his wife decide to intercede and save his life. Later, Ren arrives, but his repeated questions and the innkeeper's evasive answers make each suspect that the other is also involved in the plot to harm the general.

Ren puts up at the inn. After he has fallen asleep, the innkeeper stealthily enters the room in the dark. (The stage, however, is brightly lit.) His groping awakens Ren and a fierce struggle ensues. The comic hairbreadth misses hold the audience spellbound.

The confusion increases until at last the innkeeper's wife brings in a light and, with the help of the general, the whole misunderstanding is cleared up.

Ren Tanghui (*holding sword*) and the innkeeper in Ren's room. The table is the only prop used throughout the entire drama.

Fighting in the dark

All photos of **Crossroads** by Weng Naiqiang

Chen, who forsakes his wife and marries the emperor's sister.

Bao Zheng, a paragon of justice

QIN XIANGLIAN, THE FORSAKEN WIFE

During the Song dynasty (960-1279), there lived a poor scholar named Chen Shimei. One year, he left his home in Junzhou to go to the capital to sit for the highest imperial examination. He won the title *zhuangyuan* for the highest grade of scholar. Concealing the fact that he already had a wife and children at home, he married the emperor's sister.

After a few years, Qin Xianglian, his first wife, went to the capital with their son and daughter in search of her husband. Chen Shimei, greedy for position and wealth, pretended not to know his wife when he saw her. Later, on his birthday, when his wife disguised herself as a street singer to perform before him, he once again refused to acknowledge her. On the contrary, he sent his servant to murder her and the children. But, on hearing the deserted wife's story, the servant could not bring himself to kill them and, unable to go back to his master, took his own life instead.

Driven to desperation, Qin Xianglian presented her complaint to Bao Zheng (popularly known as Bao Gong), a most upright minister. Bao tried to persuade Chen Shimei to accept his wife and children, but Chen remained adamant. Despite the pleas of the empress dowager and Chen's second wife, the minister was determined to uphold justice and, running the risk of losing his position, had Chen executed.

Chen's wife Qin Xianglian in the guise of a street singer ▷

Photos by Eva Siao

THE
WHITE
SNAKE

Once there was a white snake who became immortal and lived in the heavens. She turned into a very beautiful woman and came back to earth again. Here she met a blue snake, a lesser immortal, who had also become a lovely maiden. She took Blue Snake as her maidservant, and the two of them set up a home in Hangzhou.

There they met a young man named Xu Xian, with whom White Snake fell in love and married.

The couple, along with their maidservant, moved to a city on the Changjiang (Yangtze River) where White Snake, now called Lady White, provided her husband with a medicine shop. As a result of her magical powers, all the medicines became especially potent; and his business in consequence prospered exceedingly.

A Buddhist abbot then warned Xu Xian that his wife was actually a snake and gave him a preparation for her to drink which would change her into her real self. When Xu Xian saw her in her old form, he simply died of fright. White

Snake then went to heaven and, despite great difficulties, brought back a medicinal herb to restore her husband to life.

Far from being grateful, Xu Xian was more scared of her than ever. He went off to the Buddhist monastery by the Changjiang where the abbot sheltered him. White Snake came and pleaded with the abbot, but to no avail. In anger, she gathered together a great army of underwater creatures to attack the monastery.

Neither side won this battle. The abbot tried to capture White Snake but failed. White Snake, too, was unable to get her husband. The abbot realized that one reason why his magical cunning had not enabled him to make his capture was that White Snake was pregnant. So he advised Xu Xian to go back and live with her until the child was born. On Xu Xian's arrival, Blue Snake was about to attack him with her sword; but White Snake held her back.

After the child was born, Xu Xian contrived, with the help of the abbot, to have White Snake revert once again to her old form and be imprisoned under the Leifeng (Thunder Peak) Pagoda by West Lake in Hangzhou. However, Blue Snake later managed to destroy the Pagoda and rescue White Snake. The two returned to heaven.

White Snake's chance encounter with Xu Xian, a young scholar

The abbot Fa Hai warns Xu about his wife's true identity.

White Snake risks her life to obtain medicinal herbs for Xu.

Xu presents the magic wine to his wife.

Blue Snake threatens to kill the heartless Xu.

White Snake in battle array, ready to fight the abbot

White Snake about to be captured by Fa Hai with his magic jar.

All photos of **White Snake** by Zhang Zudao

AUTUMN RIVER

The story concerns the love of the scholar Pan Bizheng of the Song dynasty (960-1279) and a young Buddhist nun, Chen Miaochang. Some time ago Pan had gone to stay with his aunt who is abbess of the temple where Chen lives. A romance develops and on learning about their secret meetings, the abbess immediately sends her nephew to sit for the imperial examination in the capital. He is forced to leave without saying goodbye to his sweetheart.

Chen Miaochang, dressed in a long robe and holding a duster in her hand, rushes to the riverside when she discovers her lover has already sailed down the river. She hails a passing boat in order to pursue him. On hearing the young woman's story, the boatman, a humorous old man, purposely dawdles and demands an exorbitant sum from her.

The boat sets off across the rolling waters. On stage, the actor and actress go through the movements of rising and falling with the waves as the boat skirts shallow waters, dangerous shoals or follows the sharp bends of the river. The young woman burns with anxiety hoping to catch up with her lover while the boatman tantalizes her with his jokes. In actual fact, the kindly old man feels great sympathy for her and admires her boldness in seeking her love. He rows hard in order that she may reunite with her lover as quickly as possible.

The boat gains speed with the current. It finally catches up with the young man, and the two boats sail along side by side.

Autumn River is an episode from the full-length opera *Tale of the Jade Hairpin*.

The nun and the boatman set off across the water.

Chen Miaochang, a Taoist nun ▷
Photos by Zhang Zudao

GIVING
A
PEARL
ON
RAINBOW BRIDGE

The nymph wages war to protect her happiness.

While Nymph of Sizhou and other fairies sing and dance merrily on one side of Rainbow Bridge, they meet Bei Yong, the son of the governor of Sizhou. The Nymph invites him to the palace at the bottom of the river. There they enjoy each other's company and soon become engaged. When the time comes to part, Nymph gives her treasure — a bright pearl — to Bei Yong and they reluctantly leave each other.

The governor is against this engagement. He burns incense and asks the Jade Emperor of Heaven to intervene. In order to punish Nymph for having broken the heavenly laws and fallen in love with a mortal, the Jade Emperor sends his warriors Nezha and God Erlang with some troops to subdue her.

To protect her own happiness, the dauntless Nymph wages war against the vicious foe. Although she is aided by all the sea creatures, she is overwhelmed by sheer force of numbers and defeated in the first battle.

At this crucial moment, Bei Yong risks his life to rescue her by giving back to her the pearl. Once the pearl is in her hand, Nymph, her strength now increased, turns the tables on the enemy and overpowers God Erlang and his troops. The love between Bei Yong and Nymph, having stood severe tests, becomes even deeper.

The nymph holds up her pheasant plumes in triumph.

The two lovers are happily reunited.

THE GENERAL
AND
THE MINISTER
ARE
RECONCILED

This opera is based on the accounts given in *Lian Po and Lin Xiangru* from the *Historical Records* by Sima Qian, an eminent historian and man of letters of the Western Han dynasty (206 B.C.-23 A.D.).

During the period of the Warring States (475-221 B.C.), Lin Xiangru, originally a low-ranking official in the State of Zhao, was promoted several times for his meritorious deeds and finally became prime minister. The entire country rejoiced at the good news. But General Lian Po, who had accomplished many military feats, was most unhappy about this and repeatedly provoked Lin on the streets. Although Lin was a forbearing person, he and the general could not come to terms.

Meanwhile, the country was in danger of being attacked by the neighbouring states of Qin and Qi. The King of Zhao sent a mediator to settle differences between Lin Xiangru and Lian Po. Lin, realizing that the discord between the general and himself was just what the enemy wanted, decided that they must be reconciled and was willing to take the initiative to apologize to Lian Po.

On hearing this Lian Po was greatly moved and felt deep remorse for his uncompromising attitude. Following the old Chinese custom, he took off his hat and carried a birch on his back to ask for punishment from Lin. As soon as the two met, however, they both fell to their knees clasped each other and pledged to unite and defend their country.

Bearing a birch on his back, the general (*left*) begs for punishment from the prime minister.

Photos by Zhang Zudao

MOUNT YANDANG

As the curtain rises amid the violent beating of drums and clashing of cymbals, a flurried and excited warrior with a painted face and a long black beard enters the stage. He is He Tianlong, a general of the Sui dynasty (581-618), who is retreating to Mount Yandang under the hot attack of peasant rebels led by Meng Hailong.

Darkness has fallen when Meng Hailong reaches the summit and starts his way down the other side of the mountain. He breaks through the blockade of enemy sentinels to confront He Tianlong's main forces. The sound of fighting reverberates through the mountain. Finally, He Tianlong and his men are forced to escape into the lake.

Meng Hailong finds his way there and fierce fighting continues in the water. He Tianlong's army is again driven away by the rebels and seeks refuge at Yandang Pass. Meng launches a powerful attack, shooting and killing the enemy guards with arrows. He climbs into the stronghold and wipes out the enemy.

The opera extols the courage and tenacity of the peasant rebels. Without words or singing it presents the characters and the story through acrobatic movements and mime. The magnificent, highly-skilled "fighting" offers pleasure to the audience.

He Tianlong (*right*) retreats to Mt. Yandang.

Fighting continues in the lake.

Meng Hailong leads the peasant rebels in pursuit of the enemy.

Photos by Weng Naiqiang

SELLING
WATER

A scholarly young man walks onto the stage. Brows tightly knit, he staggers along under a shoulder-pole trying hard to steady the buckets of water swinging at either end. Shamefully he cries, "Water! Water for sale!" while sadly recalling the misfortune that has befallen his family. The young man's father, a former vice-minister of war, has been thrown into jail on a false charge and all his property has been confiscated. The son and his mother can no longer afford to live in the capital. They have moved to Suzhou where they make a living by selling water.

The young man's betrothed, Huang Guiying, lives in the same town. Her fiancé's misfortune distresses her greatly and she despises her father, who plays up to those in power, for attempting to break off her engagement.

Guiying receives the sympathy of Meiying, her maid. One day Meiying persuades her mistress to take a walk in the garden. The lively Meiying sings and dances, waving her handkerchief and reaching out to stroke the branches or stooping to caress the flowers. Guiying and her maid then ascend a pavilion to admire the scenery. There they happen to see her fiancé selling water. His pitiful state brings tears to Guiying's eyes. The clever maid, on the pretext of buying water, arranges for the two lovers to have an opportunity to reaffirm their love for each other. When they part, Guiying tells her beloved to return to the garden that night to receive some money through her maid.

Selling Water is an episode from the full-length opera *Fiery Steed*.

Guiying (*left*) and her maid Meiying

The ingenious Meiying

Photos by Eva Siao

EIGHT IMMORTALS CROSSING THE SEA

This drama is about the legendary Eight Immortals, who for many centuries have enjoyed great popularity among the Chinese people. The story goes that one day, at a banquet given by the Heavenly Queen Mother, the Eight Immortals had downed too many cups of heavenly wine and became quite inebriate. When they arrived at the seashore on their way home, they were stop-

Riding the clouds from the Celestial Peach Banquet, the Eight Immortals arrive at the seaside tipsy and gay.

ped by a sea fairy who refused to let them cross the waters on the ground that they had failed to give her advance notice.

The Immortal Lu Dongbin was so drunk that he unconsciously offended the Fairy and thus created more difficulties. In an attempt to find a way out of this deadlock, each of the other seven Immortals resorted to one trick or another to get across. The wretched Lu Dongbin was left alone to humour the Fairy by admitting his wrong-doing.

To this day, *ba xian guo hai, ge xian shen tong* remains a vivid expression in current Chinese, meaning "like the eight Immortals crossing the sea, each one showing his or her special prowess".

The Sea Fairy comes to blows with the immortal Lu Dongbin.

The immortals finally admit that they are no match for the Sea Fairy.

Photos by Zhang Zudao

The Sea Fairy jibes at Zhang Guolao, another immortal.

Photos by Eva Siao

BEAUTY
DEFIES
TYRANNY

Prime Minister Zhao Gao of the Qin dynasty (221-206 B.C.) married his daughter to the son of Kuang Hong, another minister, in the hope of forming a treacherous alliance with the latter. An upright and honest official, Kuang Hong refused to lend his support and angered Zhao.

The previous emperor Qin Shi Huang, founder of the Qin, had given Kuang Hong a precious sword called the "Blade of Heaven and Earth" (*Yu Zhou Feng*) in acknowledgement of his loyalty. Zhao Gao sent his men to steal this sword and place it in the chamber of the Second Emperor.

Kuang Hong was subsequently charged with attempting to murder the emperor. Consequently, his entire family, with the exception of Zhao Gao's son-in-law who escaped, were arrested and executed. After helping her husband to escape, Zhao Gao's daughter returned to her father's home.

One day the young emperor visited the home of Zhao Gao and, noticing the beauty of his daughter, ordered that she be sent to the court to become his imperial concubine.

In desperation and with the help of her deaf-mute maidservant, the daughter feigned madness. So cleverly did she act the part that she finally managed to convince both her father and the emperor that she was truly insane. In this way she avoided the fate assigned to her.

Zhao Gao's daughter, the beauty who defies tyranny

Photos by Eva Siao

94

Zhao Gao is visibly upset as his
daughter feigns madness.

LADY SAIHUA

Taken from the Song dynasty (960-1279) saga of the Yang Generals, this is a comedy depicting of Yang Jiye's wooing of the Lady Saihua.

Saihua, daughter of the minister She Hong, is well-versed in archery and combat skills. One day when she goes hunting in the mountains, she meets Yang Jiye, son of Yang Gun and the first senior general of the Yang family. The young couple fall in love.

Unfortunately Saihua's father is so forgetful and muddle-headed that he had promised his daughter to the sons of both Yang Gun and another minister at the court. Thus, a serious dispute ensued. To find a way out, Saihua's father is obliged to follow the suggestion of his son and invite the two young suitors to a contest. He promises to let the winner claim the bride.

During the contest, Saihua herself joins the fighting and forces the one whom she doesn't love to dismount, while she pretends to be defeated by Yang Jiye, man of her own choice. However, the loser does not admit defeat. His father leads troops against She Hong; Yang Gun also comes to reason with She Hong. The quarrel between the three families turns into tangled fighting. Taking advantage of the situation, the matchmaker starts a rumour that Saihua's brother has been killed by Yang Jiye. The impulsive young woman takes up arms against the latter to avenge her brother. Jiye is forced to take refuge in a temple and finally manages to capture Saihua and takes her to the temple.

Meanwhile, She Hong and the matchmaker have run into the same temple to hide from Yang Gun, and have disguised themselves as statues of gods. There they see Yang Jiye and Saihua clear up their misunderstanding and take an oath before them to become engaged. The "statues" suddenly throw off their disguises and step down. The matchmaker apologizes to the young couple and volunteers to help arrange their wedding. She Hong makes amends by consenting to marry Saihua to her love.

Lady Saihua and the young man she loves

Lady Saihua on horseback

Photos by Eva Siao

THE
RUSE
OF THE
EMPTY CITY

This is a story from the well-known historical novel *The Three Kingdoms*. It refers to an episode in the war between the states of Shu and Wei.

The Wei general, Sima Yi, sent his army to occupy the strategic places that commanded the important area of Hanzhong.

Zhuge Liang, the Shu strategist, ordered his army to come up and especially hold Jieting. But Commander Ma Su did not follow his order, the troops did not arrive and Zhuge Liang was left in the lurch. Sima Yi occupied Jieting and moved

on to Xicheng where Zhuge Liang had his headquarters.

Zhuge Liang had been warned by the old guards at the city gates of the imminent arrival of the enemy. Throwing the city gates wide open, he mounted the city wall and pretended to amuse himself with his lute and wine.

On his arrival Sima Yi was puzzled by the sight and thought that surely an ambush had been set. Zhuge Liang had a great reputation for such. So Sima Yi retreated for forty li and waited.

During this time Zhuge Liang waited for the forces of Zhao Yun, another commander, to arrive. After Zhao Yun appeared, Sima Yi realized that he had been outwitted and in consequence beat a retreat.

Zhuge Liang afterwards executed Ma Su, who had disobeyed commands at a critical moment. At the same time he blamed himself for having wrongly trusted this subordinate.

General Sima Yi (*centre*) is puzzled and dares not enter the city gate. Zhuge Liang sits atop the wall.

by Zhang Shuicheng

Zhuge Liang, noted military strategist of the State of Shu.

Sima Yi, general of the State of Wei.

Photos by Eva Siao

The young scholar and the nun *in Autumn River*

ISBN 7-80005-090-4/J.019

京 剧 画 册

编　辑　马　节
美术编辑　李玉鸿
摄　影　叶　华　等

※

新世界出版社出版（北京）
1202印刷厂印刷
中国国际图书贸易总公司发行
（中国北京车公庄西路21号）
北京邮政信箱第399号　邮政编码100044
1984年第一版　1989年第二次印刷
编号：（英）85223—137
02300
85—E—219 P